Original title:

The Love Catalyst

Author: Claudia Kuma

ISBN HARDBACK: 978-9916-87-339-7

ISBN PAPERBACK: 978-9916-87-340-3

ISBN EBOOK: 978-9916-87-341-0

A Woven Dreamscape

In twilight's glow, whispers hum,
A tapestry of dreams begun.
Threads of silver, strands of gold,
Stories waiting to be told.

Stars weave patterns in the night,
Guiding hearts with gentle light.
Clouds drift softly, secrets shared,
In this haven, souls are bared.

Fields of wonder, deep and wide,
Where hopes and fears can safely bide.
Mirrored lakes reflect the skies,
Truths emerge, no need for lies.

With each heartbeat, colors dance,
In this realm of pure romance.
Awake or dream, it matters not,
A woven dreamscape, love is wrought.

Moments Between Us

In the quiet dusk we find,
Whispers soft, hearts entwined.
Every glance a fleeting spark,
Time slows down, a fiery arc.

Laughter dances in the air,
Memories linger, sweet and rare.
In this space, we both reside,
Moments cherished, side by side.

Serenade of Souls

Underneath the moon's embrace,
Melodies weave in sacred space.
Every note a tale retold,
Echoes of love, vibrant and bold.

Together, we create a song,
Harmonies that can't go wrong.
With every heartbeat's gentle sway,
Our spirits dance, come what may.

Cauldron of Yearning

Deep within the heart's desire,
Burning brightly, a fierce fire.
Whispers call from shadows near,
Yearning souls, we sip our fear.

A cauldron filled with dreams untold,
Hopes that shimmer, bright and bold.
In the night, our visions blend,
Magic stirs where passions mend.

Unveiling Hidden Passions

Behind the veil, the secrets lie,
Embers spark as shadows fly.
Every touch a silent plea,
Unveiling truths, just you and me.

In the twilight's tender glow,
Passions bloom, then ebb and flow.
Together we explore the night,
Souls ignited, taking flight.

Whispers of Affection

In quiet moments, hearts collide,
Soft words dance, as feelings guide.
Gentle smiles beneath the trees,
Love speaks softly, carried by the breeze.

Hands entwined in twilight’s glow,
Dreams awaken, seeds we sow.
Each glance a promise, a tender thread,
A chorus of love, silently said.

Bonds Beyond Touch

In worlds apart, our spirits meet,
Silent echoes, a rhythm sweet.
No distance can dim our bright flame,
In every heartbeat, I call your name.

Time may wane, yet love remains,
A tether strong through joys and pains.
In laughter shared and sorrows borne,
The light of us, forever sworn.

Sparks in the Shadows

In the dark where secrets lie,
Flickers dance with every sigh.
Hidden glances, a knowing spark,
Connection blooms in the silent dark.

A touch that lingers, electric, rare,
Breathless moments in whispered air.
Together we're a song, softly sung,
In the hush of night, where love is young.

Embrace of Euphoria

In vivid dreams, we come alive,
A world of color, where passions thrive.
Every heartbeat ignites the air,
Lost in laughter, we're free of care.

Twilight dances on our skin,
With every word, new worlds begin.
Wrapped in joy, our spirits soar,
A euphoric love, forevermore.

The Bloom of Togetherness

In the garden where we stand,
Petals brush like gentle hands.
Colors blend, no shade in sight,
Unified in pure delight.

Through the seasons, roots entwine,
Ever growing, yours and mine.
In the sun, our laughter plays,
Blooming bright in countless ways.

With every drop of morning dew,
Whispers tell of love so true.
In the silence, flowers sigh,
Together, we reach for the sky.

Moments gather, memories grow,
In this space, our spirits flow.
With hearts open and voices clear,
Togetherness dispels the fear.

Fusion of Kindred Spirits

Two souls meet on paths unknown,
In their hearts, a warmth has grown.
Like the stars that pierce the night,
Shining bright, they share their light.

Voices blend in harmony,
Creating sweet symphony.
Together they dance through the day,
In each other's arms, they sway.

Though the world may twist and bend,
Their bond will never come to end.
With laughter echoing through time,
In every challenge, they will climb.

With every breath, they intertwine,
A tapestry of hearts divine.
In the silence, they find peace,
In this fusion, love's increase.

Harmonies of the Heart

Softly played on evening strings,
Whispers of what true love brings.
In each note, a memory glows,
A melody that ever flows.

Through the storm and quiet days,
Hearts compose in countless ways.
In the rhythm, pulses beat,
Together, every moment sweet.

With a glance, they understand,
Life’s great dance, a gentle hand.
In the shadows, light abounds,
In their laughter, hope resounds.

As the moon begins to rise,
In its glow, their spirits fly.
Harmonies that never part,
The music is their beating heart.

Unraveling Boundless Ties

Threads entwine, both old and new,
Binding hearts in every hue.
With each pull, the fabric weaves,
A story spun of hopes and dreams.

Through the distance, bonds will stretch,
In every memory, we'll etch.
Side by side, though worlds apart,
Unraveling, we share one heart.

In the silence, truth finds voice,
In the dark, we make our choice.
Every moment, every tear,
Ties unravel, but love is near.

With open arms, we face the dawn,
In each heartbeat, we carry on.
Boundless ties that won’t be broken,
With every word, love's softly spoken.

Illuminate the Shadows

In the silence of the night,
Whispers of hope take flight,
Casting light on what we fear,
Breaking through, the path is clear.

Stars above begin to glow,
Guiding us where peace may flow,
With each step, the dark will fade,
Illumination softly laid.

Embrace the warmth, let it grow,
In our hearts, a steady flow,
Every shadow finds its light,
Together, we will shine so bright.

The Pulse of Affection

In the heartbeat of a glance,
Underneath the starlit dance,
Feel the rhythm, soft and true,
Bound together, me and you.

Every word, a gentle breeze,
Whispers float with perfect ease,
In this moment, hearts align,
Love's sweet pulse, forever mine.

With each breath, connection grows,
Through the highs and through the lows,
In this truth, we find our way,
The pulse of affection, here to stay.

Bridges of Connection

From one heart to another's beat,
Building bridges, strong and sweet,
Crossing rivers of despair,
Finding hope in softest air.

Hand in hand, we step as one,
Together under the same sun,
With each stride, we weave our thread,
A tapestry where love is spread.

Through the echoes of our past,
Connections forged to ever last,
In the laughter and the tears,
Bridges built to conquer fears.

Sweet Currents of Unity

In the depths of flowing streams,
Unity ignites our dreams,
Sweet currents guide us as we go,
Together, we create the flow.

Every voice a note, a sound,
In harmony, our roots are found,
As the waters intertwine,
United we, like branches, shine.

Beneath the surface, life will thrive,
In our hearts, we feel alive,
In the dance of give and take,
Sweet currents for connection's sake.

Rhapsody of Connection

In the quiet of the night,
Hearts beat in sweet accord,
We find our shared delight,
With every whispered word.

Eyes meet in sacred space,
A glance that speaks so loud,
In this beautiful embrace,
Together we are proud.

Hands intertwine so tight,
Binding souls like a song,
In the warmth of the light,
Where we both belong.

A melody that will stay,
Forever intertwined,
In this rhapsody we play,
A love that’s so aligned.

Fireflies in Twilight

Glimmers dance in the air,
Fireflies weave through the night,
Their glow a secret flare,
A symphony of light.

As shadows blend and bend,
We chase the fleeting spark,
In twilight's soft suspend,
A world that's warm and dark.

Moments drift like the breeze,
In laughter and soft sighs,
Holding on to the ease,
Beneath the starry skies.

Together, we will roam,
With every flicker, a dream,
In this enchanted home,
Where hope and wonder gleam.

A Cascade of Dreams

Waves of thoughts gently flow,
In currents of the night,
Like rivers, we will go,
With stars guiding our flight.

Each vision, a spark of light,
A cascade of pure desire,
In the embrace of the night,
We’ll rise ever higher.

Imagination's sweet flight,
Unfurling in the calm,
A tapestry of insight,
Its threads woven in balm.

Together, we will chase,
The dreams that fill our soul,
In this beautiful space,
Where heart and mind are whole.

Ties that Bind

In the fabric of our days,
Threads of laughter and tears,
We weave through life's maze,
Building bonds through the years.

With every shared embrace,
Moments stitched with care,
In this warm, sacred space,
There's love everywhere.

Through trials, we have grown,
United, we stand tall,
In each heart, we have sown,
The strength to rise, not fall.

Together we'll endure,
As ties that bind us tight,
In a world that feels unsure,
Together, we ignite.

Unwritten Conversations

In whispers lost, words intertwine,
Thoughts unspoken, dreams align.
Moments hang in the silent air,
Between us, a bond we share.

Eyes meet softly, stories bloom,
In the quiet, love finds room.
Fingers brush like gentle rain,
In the hush, there's no more pain.

Laughter dances, shadows play,
Yet in silence, we long to say.
Every glance, a novel's start,
In this space, we guard our heart.

Unwritten tales in twilight's glow,
In the pause, our feelings flow.
A canvas blank, waiting for ink,
In unwritten words, we think.

Seasons of Yearning

Spring whispers soft, life anew,
Blossoms blush in morning dew.
Every petal tells a tale,
Of love that lingers, never pale.

Summer's heat, desires burn,
Longing hearts in turns we learn.
Golden rays on skin ignite,
In every glance, there's sheer delight.

Autumn's chill, the leaves descend,
Fleeting moments, time to bend.
Whispers of a love once bright,
In the dusk, we seek the light.

Winter's breath, a silent plea,
Yearning hearts in harmony.
In the stillness, hope survives,
Four seasons hold the love that thrives.

Caught in Your Orbit

Around you, my heart takes flight,
Gravity pulls, holding tight.
In a dance of cosmic chance,
We twirl beneath the stars' romance.

Your laughter lights my darkest skies,
In your gaze, the universe lies.
With every word, you weave a spell,
In your orbit, I wish to dwell.

Time suspends, a fleeting glance,
In this moment, lost in trance.
Celestial sparks that brightly glow,
In your presence, time moves slow.

Caught in this beautiful embrace,
In your rhythm, I find my place.
Like planets near, we align so true,
In this vast expanse, it's just me and you.

Fables of the Heart

Once upon a moonlit dream,
Hearts entwined like flowing stream.
Every chapter, a tale unfolds,
In whispered secrets, love is told.

Brave knights and gentle hearts, too,
In woven fables made for two.
With dreams like lanterns shining bright,
We pen our story, day and night.

Adventures found in every sigh,
Beneath the stars, we learn to fly.
In the pages, our laughter rings,
As two souls dance on fragile wings.

Through time and trials, we shall part,
Yet in the end, it’s love's true art.
For every fable we impart,
Is but a song of the heart.

Whirlwind of Emotions

In the tempest of my heart,
Feelings swirl and spin,
Joy and sorrow intertwined,
A dance that won't begin.

Thoughts collide like thunder,
Whispers go unheard,
In this storm of the soul,
Every feeling blurred.

Moments flash like lightning,
Flickering, they fade,
Lost in a fleeting chaos,
In shadows, I parade.

Yet within the tumult,
A calm can sometimes break,
In the eye of the storm,
A promise yet to make.

Journeys of Affection

Hand in hand, we wander,
Through valleys green and wide,
With every step together,
Our hearts a faithful guide.

The road is often winding,
With mountains to ascend,
But each slope brings us closer,
Love that will not bend.

In laughter and in silence,
Memories softly glow,
A tapestry of moments,
In the ebb and flow.

Together in the twilight,
With stars to light our way,
Our journey's just beginning,
In the dawn of day.

Reflections in Your Eyes

In the mirror of your gaze,
I see stories unfold,
Whispers of a thousand dreams,
In colors bright and bold.

Depths of endless oceans,
Soft waves upon the shore,
Every glance a secret,
I long to know much more.

Time pauses for a moment,
As worlds collide in spark,
A universe within you,
Illuminated dark.

Caught in this reflection,
I find both peace and strife,
Lost and yet discovered,
In the essence of your life.

Bonds of Forgotten Time

In the attic of my memory,
Dusty dreams reside,
Fragments of our laughter,
Where time has softly died.

Whispers from the shadows,
Echo through the years,
A tapestry of moments,
Woven with our tears.

While footsteps fade to silence,
And faces turn to night,
The bonds we forged in daylight,
Are forever held in sight.

Though seasons may be changing,
And paths divide anew,
Those memories linger sweetly,
A love that's tried and true.

Flames of Shared Dreams

In twilight's glow, our hopes ignite,
Whispers of wishes take their flight.
Together we build, brick by brick,
A castle of dreams, bold and thick.

Through shadows cast by doubts and fears,
We chase the dawn, through laughter and tears.
With every spark, our journey grows,
Kindling love that endlessly flows.

Hearts entwined, we stand as one,
Chasing the rays of a rising sun.
In every trial, we find our way,
Flames of dreams guide us each day.

Mosaic of Intimacy

In fragments small, our stories blend,
Colors of love, they twist and bend.
Every glance, a piece of art,
Together we form a beating heart.

Soft touches weave a tender thread,
Cocooned in warmth, where dreams are fed.
We share our secrets, layer by layer,
Creating a bond, fragile yet rare.

In silence thick, our spirits soar,
With every heartbeat, we explore.
A dance of souls, so rich, so free,
This mosaic blooms in harmony.

Journeys of the Heart

Along the path, we wander wide,
Side by side, with love as guide.
Each step we take, a tale unfolds,
Of whispers soft and hands we hold.

Through valleys low and mountains high,
We'll face the storms, together try.
In every moment, joy and strife,
We shape the journey, bound to life.

With compass drawn by dreams anew,
Boundless horizons, skies so blue.
With every heartbeat, worlds align,
Journeys together, yours and mine.

Synergy of Kindness

In gentle acts, we find our grace,
A simple smile, a warm embrace.
In every moment, hearts conspire,
To weave a world that lifts us higher.

Through kindness sown, we build the thread,
Of hope and love; in hearts, it's spread.
A ripple's touch can spark a flame,
Uniting souls, we praise the name.

In unity, our strength will grow,
With every seed, goodwill we sow.
Together we rise, a radiant shine,
Creating bonds that intertwine.

Footsteps of Devotion

In quiet moments, whispers rise,
A path adorned with gentle sighs.
With every step, a promise laid,
In shadows of the love we've made.

Through trials faced, we stand as one,
United beneath the warming sun.
Each heartbeat echoes, strong and true,
In footsteps borne from me to you.

In gardens blooming, we shall tread,
With fervent hopes and words unsaid.
The bond we share defies the night,
Illuminated by love's pure light.

As stars align with perfect grace,
Our souls entwined in time and space.
Together forged, hand in hand,
In devotion's realm, we firmly stand.

Unfurling Hearts

In the dawn's embrace, petals spread,
Gentle whispers, softly said.
With every glance, our spirits soar,
Unfurling dreams we can't ignore.

Through vibrant colors, passions bloom,
In every shadow, love finds room.
A canvas painted, hearts entwined,
In brilliant hues, our souls aligned.

As winds of change begin to play,
We sail through life, come what may.
With every memory carved in gold,
Unfurling stories waiting to be told.

In sacred spaces, we reside,
With open hearts, no need to hide.
Together we dance to life's sweet tune,
Unfurling hearts beneath the moon.

Resonance of Two

In symphonies of shared delight,
Harmonies blend within the night.
With every beat, our spirits glide,
In melodies where love abides.

Two souls entwined, a perfect chord,
In gentle rhythms, hearts restored.
With laughter ringing, echoes grow,
A resonance that time shall know.

Through every storm, we find our way,
In whispered dreams that softly sway.
As raindrops dance on window panes,
Our love persists, through joys and pains.

In quiet corners, secrets bloom,
In every heartbeat, love's perfume.
Together we craft our destined song,
In resonance where we belong.

Language of the Heart

In gaze that lingers, words unspoken,
A language soft, yet never broken.
With every sigh, a tale begins,
In rhythms sweet, our love now spins.

With tender glances, secrets found,
In silence deep, our souls are bound.
In every heartbeat, stories weave,
The language shared, we both believe.

Through time we travel, hand in hand,
In whispered dreams, we understand.
Each moment cherished, never lost,
In love's embrace, we count the cost.

With every touch, a symphony,
In breath and heart, a harmony.
Together we write, a timeless art,
In the lovely language of the heart.

Luminous Bonds

In twilight's glow, we share a dream,
Two souls entwined, a brilliant beam.
With laughter bright, we light the night,
In every glance, our hearts take flight.

Through storms we stand, a steady force,
A river wide, we chart our course.
With hands held tight, we face the dawn,
Together forged, forever drawn.

A Tapestry of Embrace

Threads of laughter weave the night,
In every hug, the world feels right.
Colors blend in warm embrace,
A tapestry of joy we trace.

With every heartbeat, stories told,
In gentle warmth, our dreams unfold.
Like stars that spark in endless skies,
Our bond, a gift that never dies.

The Essence of Together

In quiet moments, peace we find,
Two hearts as one, forever aligned.
With whispers soft like morning light,
Together we conquer day and night.

Each step we take, a rhythm true,
In every path, I walk with you.
Through valleys low and mountains high,
Our essence blends, we touch the sky.

Windswept Whispers

Beneath the trees, where shadows play,
The winds bring forth what words can't say.
Our secrets carried, lost in flight,
In nature's song, we find delight.

With every breeze, I feel you near,
Your laughter dances, sweet and clear.
In every sigh, the world abounds,
In windswept whispers, love resounds.

Whispers of Connection

In quiet moments we convene,
Whispers soft like silk unseen.
Hearts align in gentle grace,
Across the void, we find our place.

Threads of fate weave us tight,
Guiding souls through the night.
Silent glances, a knowing smile,
In your presence, I walk a mile.

Every heartbeat speaks your name,
In this dance, we're not the same.
Yet harmony in every sigh,
A bond unbreakable, you and I.

Like shadows cast in morning light,
We linger close, a shared delight.
With each whisper, our spirits soar,
In connection, we are evermore.

Sparks in the Night

Beneath the stars, a fire ignites,
A moment shared, our souls in flight.
Fleeting glances, quickened breath,
In the dark, love conquers death.

Fingertips brush, electric thrill,
In the silence, hearts stand still.
Every laugh, a flicker bright,
Together we burn, a beautiful sight.

The moon bears witness, soft and round,
As whispers blend with the night's sweet sound.
With each promise, a flame we stoke,
In the shadows, love's tender smoke.

When shadows fade and dawn arrives,
In the light, our essence thrives.
Every spark a memory, warm and right,
Forever we'll chase these sparks of night.

Heartstrings Entwined

In a garden where dreams bloom bright,
Two hearts dance in morning light.
With gentle hands, we shape our fate,
In this love, we find our state.

Every glance a secret plea,
In every moment, you're near me.
Entwined like vines, we grow and climb,
In the symphony of souls, we rhyme.

Through the storms and gentle rain,
We bear the weight, we feel the pain.
Yet in the tether of every sigh,
Our heartstrings hum, a lullaby.

Together weaving the time we share,
In this tapestry, we lay bare.
With each heartbeat, our truth aligns,
Two souls forever, heartstrings entwined.

Alchemy of Affection

In the forge where passions meet,
We craft our dreams, a rhythmic beat.
Molten rays from hearts aflame,
Transforming shadows, calling names.

With every glance, we shape and mold,
A tale of love, a story told.
In tender whispers, gold is spun,
Alchemy of us has just begun.

Through trials faced, we find our way,
Turning lead to light, come what may.
In every smile, the world refines,
This magic born in shifting lines.

Cloaked in moments, soft and bright,
We conjure love beneath the night.
As elements blend, our spirits sign,
In the alchemy of affection, we shine.

Tides of Tenderness

In whispers soft as summer rain,
We find a place where hearts remain.
A gentle touch, a knowing glance,
In moonlit nights, we weave our dance.

The tide will rise, the tide will fall,
Yet in your arms, I have it all.
Each wave a promise, sweet and clear,
In this embrace, I hold you near.

With every ebb, a story told,
Of love that never grows too old.
Together, we will brave the sea,
Bound by this tender mystery.

So let us drift, let dreams unfold,
In tides of warmth, together bold.
Your heartbeat sings a melody,
A symphony of you and me.

Chasing Stardust Together

Under the vast and starlit sky,
We chase the dreams that soar so high.
With every step, our laughter flies,
In the night glow, our spirits rise.

Hand in hand, we wander wide,
Through cosmic paths, with joy as guide.
Each twinkle sparks a wish anew,
In this adventure, just us two.

The universe sings, a soft refrain,
As we embrace the heart and pain.
In fleeting moments, time stands still,
Together chasing every thrill.

So let us dance on celestial beams,
With love that flows like whispered dreams.
In the tapestry of night we weave,
Chasing stardust, we believe.

Dance of Intimacy

In shadows deep, we find our way,
A silent beat, the words we play.
With closeness wrapped in gentle grace,
We breathe the warmth of our embrace.

Each glance ignites the fire inside,
In perfect harmony, we confide.
Our bodies move like whispered tunes,
In dance, we banish all the gloom.

The world fades out; it's just us here,
Lost in a rhythm, loud and clear.
With every step, we build our song,
In intimacy, we both belong.

So let us sway, the night is ours,
Underneath the glowing stars.
In this dance, our hearts align,
Forever yours, forever mine.

Threads of Destiny

With every stitch, a story spun,
In threads of fate, two hearts are one.
We weave the fabric of our days,
In colors bright, in gentle ways.

The loom of life pulls tight and loose,
Each moment shared, a sweet excuse.
With love as thread, we bind our souls,
In woven dreams, we reach our goals.

Through trials faced and joys embraced,
In patterns rich, our love is graced.
The tapestry tells of our fight,
In every hue, it shines so bright.

So let us sew with needle fine,
In threads of destiny, entwined.
Together, we will craft our fate,
In love's design, we celebrate.

Sea of Infinite Possibilities

Waves crash gently on the shore,
Echoing dreams from days of yore.
The horizon whispers tales untold,
In the vast depths where visions unfold.

Sails unfurl into the morning light,
Carving paths through endless flight.
Each ripple a chance, a brand new way,
Guiding hearts to seize the day.

Beneath the surface, secrets sleep,
In currents of hope, our thoughts we keep.
Explore the depths, let courage rise,
In this boundless sea, our spirits fly.

So take a leap, let go of the shore,
For the sea of life holds so much more.
In every wave, in every swell,
Lie infinite possibilities to dwell.

Palette of Emotions

Crimson whispers of love’s embrace,
Brushstrokes dance with tender grace.
Azure blues of sorrow’s song,
In every hue, our hearts belong.

Golden rays of joy ignite,
Painting landscapes warm and bright.
Emerald greens of hope arise,
In the canvas, our dreams disguise.

Violet shadows of fear take flight,
Yet lavender brings the calm of night.
Each color tells a story deep,
A palette where our spirits sweep.

So gather your brush, let passions flow,
In this sea of feelings, let your heart show.
We are artists with tales to share,
In the palette of life, we find our care.

A Moment Captured

A fleeting glance, the world stands still,
Time folds gently, a heart to fill.
Amongst the chaos, clarity blooms,
In a breath’s pause, destiny looms.

Laughter echoes through the air,
Captured joy, an eternal flare.
Soft whispers brush against our skin,
In this brief pause, we begin to spin.

Golden sunsets paint the sky,
Each moment a gift as time slips by.
In snapshots of love, we find our song,
In the fabric of time, where we belong.

Hold it close, this fleeting spark,
For in these seconds, we leave our mark.
Every heartbeat, a tale to weave,
In the moment captured, we truly believe.

The Unfinished Story

Pages turn, yet tales remain,
In ink of hope, through joy and pain.
Chapters linger in shadows cast,
Whispers of futures, tangled with past.

Each character breathes with dreams untold,
In the quiet moments, the heart is bold.
A plot twist waits just out of sight,
In the unfinished manuscript of light.

Unwritten lines dance in our heads,
A tapestry woven of words and threads.
With every stroke, new paths we chart,
In the unwritten, lies the art.

So pen your dreams, let your spirit soar,
For life's true tale is forever more.
In the unfinished, find your story,
In woven fragments, claim your glory.

Traces of an Enchantment

In twilight's glow, memories flicker,
Whispers of dreams laced in the air.
Softly they dance, shadows grow thicker,
Leaving a trace of magic rare.

With every sigh, the night unfolds,
Stars weave stories, secrets unfurl.
In echoes of laughter, the past still holds,
Mysteries wrapped in a silken whirl.

The moonlight paints hearts with a brush,
Embracing the stillness, silence speaks.
In the quiet, there's a gentle rush,
Unveiling the love that softly peaks.

An enchantment lingers, soft and clear,
Binding the moments, timeless and true.
In every heartbeat, it reappears,
A dance of the soul, forever new.

Portraits of Passion

Brushstrokes capture a fervent flame,
Colors of longing on canvas displayed.
Eyes locked in silence, whisper your name,
Every detail carefully laid.

In every gesture, a story unfolds,
The warmth of embrace, a dance of two.
Through laughter and tears, love never grows old,
Despite the trials that they both knew.

Moments in time, forever confined,
Each portrait a glimpse of what once was.
In shadows and light, a tale we find,
A testament crafted with love's pure cause.

With every color, the heart expresses,
The beauty of passion, wild and rare.
Through strokes of the brush, it never suppresses,
A timeless reminder of love laid bare.

Navigating the Unknown

A compass points to paths unseen,
Whispers of fate guide each small stride.
Through fog and shadow, a journey keen,
With trust as our ship, we sail the tide.

Uncharted waters call and entice,
Unfamiliar shores beckon our quest.
With courage as anchor, we pay the price,
Finding our way, feeling truly blessed.

The stars above, our guides in the dark,
Every heartbeat a rhythm, a chance.
In silence we share, igniting the spark,
As we forge ahead in life's bold dance.

With each step forward, we face the dawn,
Carving our path through dusk’s sweet embrace.
In the vast unknown, hope carries on,
Finding our way in this endless space.

Blossoms of Yearning

In the garden of dreams where wishes bloom,
Petals unfurl with secrets untold.
Fragrant whispers in evening's loom,
Softly they beckon, tender and bold.

Each blossom sways to a silent song,
A dance of emotions, vibrant and bright.
In shades of longing, hearts grow strong,
Painting the night with colors of light.

A tapestry woven, the fabric of time,
Threads of desire entwined with hope.
In the silence of night, love's sweet rhyme,
Guides the weary and helps them cope.

Among the petals, yearnings reside,
Dreams take root, embracing the day.
In the hearts of the brave, they cannot hide,
Blossoms of yearning forever will sway.

Heartbeats in Harmony

In quiet whispers of the night,
Two souls connect, a shared delight.
Each heartbeat echoes, soft and clear,
A rhythmic dance, drawing near.

Through laughter, tears, the moments flow,
In silent vows, together they grow.
A symphony played in gentle tones,
Unity binds, never alone.

When shadows fall, they will not part,
For love's embrace ignites the heart.
In every glance, a story told,
A magic woven, rich and bold.

As daybreak paints the skies anew,
Hand in hand, they journey through.
With every heartbeat, love expands,
In harmony, they make their plans.

Emblems of Devotion

Beneath the stars, a promise gleams,
In every glance, love’s purest dreams.
With each soft touch, a bond is formed,
A sacred trust, forever warmed.

Through trials faced, their spirits rise,
In silence shared, no need for lies.
A treasure found in simple things,
In laughter’s joy, devotion sings.

In fleeting moments, time stands still,
As hearts entwine, they find their will.
Emblems crafted from pain and joy,
In union strong, no fear to destroy.

With every breath, they vow to stay,
In love's embrace, they find their way.
Together always, hand in hand,
In every heartbeat, a promised land.

Canvas of Emotions

Colors blend on life's vast stage,
Each stroke a tale, turning the page.
From dark to light, the hues will grow,
A masterpiece in every flow.

With each sunrise, new shades appear,
A palette rich, both bold and clear.
Brush of laughter, tear of pain,
In every canvas, love's refrain.

The heart speaks loud, with shades unseen,
In every flick, a silent dream.
Together weaving, side by side,
Creating worlds where hearts abide.

In artful strokes, life's lessons learned,
With every fire, a passion burned.
A tapestry of feelings wide,
In this grand canvas, love's our guide.

Harmony of the Unseen

In gentle breezes, secrets sigh,
A melody that whispers by.
In quiet moments, peace is found,
A soft embrace, a sacred sound.

Through tangled paths, they walk as one,
Each step aligned, a race well run.
In every silence, truths unfold,
A symphony of hearts, bold and gold.

The unseen threads that weave our fate,
In love's embrace, we resonate.
With every heartbeat, spirits soar,
In harmony with all, we explore.

When darkness comes, they hold the light,
In shared conviction, hearts ignite.
Together strong, in peace they dwell,
In harmony of unseen, they tell.

A Tapestry of Love

In threads of gold and crimson hue,
We weave our dreams, both old and new.
With every stitch, our hearts align,
A tapestry where souls entwine.

Through seasons bright and shadows deep,
Our bond, a promise, forever to keep.
In every tear, a joy reborn,
Love's gentle touch, like petals worn.

Melodies of Affection

Soft whispers dance upon the breeze,
In perfect tune, they aim to please.
With every laugh, a note so sweet,
Our hearts compose a rhythmic beat.

In quiet moments, harmonies bloom,
As stars align in twilight's gloom.
These gentle sounds, a lover's song,
In melodies, our hearts belong.

Underneath the Moonlit Veil

Beneath the stars, in silver light,
We share our secrets, pure and bright.
The cool night air, a soft embrace,
In shadows deep, we find our place.

With every glance, the world fades away,
As whispers of love begin to play.
In moonlit paths, our dreams unwind,
Two souls entwined, forever aligned.

The Color of Longing

In shades of blue, my heart does ache,
A quiet wish, a gentle wake.
With every dawn, I feel the pull,
The color of longing, deep and full.

With strokes of passion, not of despair,
I paint my hopes in the open air.
Each brush, a promise, soft yet strong,
In hues of yearning, I find where I belong.

Boundless Horizons of Us

In the dawn's soft glow, we rise,
Chasing dreams under endless skies.
Every step a new embrace,
Together, we find our rightful place.

Winds of change whisper our name,
Through valleys vast, we stake our claim.
Hearts alight with fervent trust,
With every moment, it's a must.

Side by side, we face the tide,
In this journey, we confide.
Boundless horizons, endless seas,
With every beat, we craft our peace.

Every sunset paints our tale,
In laughter's dance, we prevail.
Hand in hand, our spirits soar,
In the symphony of evermore.

Veil of Enchantment.

Beneath the moon's luminous kiss,
Whispers linger in the abyss.
A tapestry woven with stars,
In this night, we find who we are.

Mystic shadows softly gleam,
In the silence, we dare to dream.
Caught in the magic of the hour,
Two souls entwined in a sacred power.

The twilight sings a haunting tune,
Every heartbeat, a fleeting swoon.
In the dance of the silken air,
We weave our dreams without a care.

As dawn approaches, we hold tight,
Wrapped in the veil of soft starlight.
With every whisper, the world fades,
In our hearts, the enchantment stays.

Heartstrings Entwined

In the garden where laughter blooms,
We trace the path in whispered rooms.
Every glance, a spark ignites,
Two souls align on moonlit nights.

Fingers brush in tender grace,
In the quiet, love finds its place.
A melody only we know,
In unison, our spirits flow.

Through trials faced and joys we find,
In every heartbeat, love's defined.
Woven threads of hope and trust,
In this bond, we're forever gust.

As seasons change, we stand as one,
With laughter echoing like the sun.
Heartstrings entwined, forever thine,
In this dance of life, truly divine.

Chemistry of Souls

In the quiet, a spark ignites,
Two hearts collide on starry nights.
A glance shared, electric thrill,
In this moment, we feel the chill.

Words unspoken, yet understood,
In the chaos, we find our good.
With every laugh, a bond does grow,
In this dance, our spirits flow.

The universe spins in delight,
As we navigate through the night.
Drawing closer, like planets align,
In the chemistry of souls, so divine.

Every heartbeat syncs in time,
A melody sweet, a perfect rhyme.
Together, we write our own fate,
In love's embrace, it’s never too late.

Notes in the Margins

Whispers scribbled in the page,
Ink drips like silent rage.
Thoughts that dance on faded lines,
Secrets trapped in soft designs.

Footprints of the mind's retreat,
Lost in echoes, bittersweet.
Fragments of a life once bright,
Carved in shadows, kissed by light.

Fleeting moments, paused in ink,
Silent musings make us think.
Boundless worlds in tiny space,
Time's embrace, a soft embrace.

In margins where our dreams reside,
Boundless wisdom, hope, and pride.
The past lingers, the future gleams,
Life unfolds in whispered dreams.

Heart's Invisible Thread

An unseen force pulls me near,
Binding souls, intertwining fear.
A gentle touch, a knowing glance,
Written love in fate's own dance.

Through trials faced and shadows cast,
Our hearts entwined, forever fast.
Echoes of laughter fill the air,
Woven tight, a bond so rare.

In every heartbeat, stories bloom,
A tapestry dispels the gloom.
Each thread a tale, a life once led,
Through joy and sorrow, widely spread.

Together we rise, together we fall,
Pulled by the thread that binds us all.
Invisible, yet oh so strong,
In love's embrace, we both belong.

Unfolding Stories

Pages crisp with tales untold,
Whispers shared in shadows bold.
Fingers trace the lines of fate,
Moments captured, hearts await.

Each story breathes, a pulse of light,
Flickering like stars at night.
Memories wrapped in fragile hues,
Life's quilt stitched with vibrant views.

Time flows freely, bends and curves,
In every twist, the heart observes.
Unwritten paths demand to be,
These tales of love, wild and free.

With every turn, a lesson learned,
From ashes, bright flames are burned.
We are the authors, pen in hand,
Crafting futures from dreams we've planned.

Diaries of Desire

Ink spills on pages bare,
Each word a wish, each line a prayer.
Heartbeat echoing in the void,
Dreams collected and enjoyed.

Whispers drift like autumn leaves,
Tales of longing, heart believes.
In every wish, a dance of fate,
Soaked in hope, inscribed in fate.

Secrets wrapped in velvet night,
Passion ignites, a flickering light.
Unveiled truths in every breath,
Awakened desires, not far from death.

The heart writes on, while shadows play,
Each desire a price to pay.
In diaries lined with dreams anew,
A journey carved for me and you.

Echoes of a Shared Soul

In whispers soft, the shadows dwell,
Two hearts entwined, a secret spell.
Through laughter's light and sorrow's tone,
Together we find, we're never alone.

The stars above, they shine so bright,
Guiding our steps, through darkest night.
In every pause, a thrum of fate,
Echoes of love, we celebrate.

Moments shared, like fleeting sighs,
In every glance, a world that flies.
Through trials faced, we stand as one,
A melody sung, a journey begun.

With every beat, our souls align,
In the tapestry of time, divine.
We'll weave our dreams, a vibrant scroll,
Forever bound, echoing our soul.

The Fire That Ignites

In twilight's glow, a spark appears,
A flicker bright, igniting fears.
With kindling hearts, we fan the flame,
Each whispered wish, a lover's name.

The dance of flames a fervent trance,
In every move, a fleeting chance.
With passion's heat, our spirits soar,
Twined in the fire, forevermore.

Through storms and winds, our blaze endures,
With warmth so pure, a love that cures.
In shadows cast, our light shines through,
Together we burn, forever true.

In radiant heat, our souls ignite,
Two hearts alight, in the darkest night.
A furnace strong, with hope we fight,
The fire of love, a guiding light.

Dance of Desires

In the moonlight, our bodies sway,
A rhythm set, come what may.
With every glance, a subtle tease,
In this dance, our hearts appease.

The music calls, enticing dreams,
In the silence, desire beams.
Twists and turns, we lose control,
Two souls entwined, a single goal.

With every step, a promise made,
In this moment, we're unafraid.
The world fades out, just you and me,
In this dance, we both are free.

As shadows play and night unfolds,
Our story whispered, gently told.
An eternal dance, forever ours,
As we twirl beneath the stars.

Threads of Heartbeats

In quiet spaces, love doth weave,
Threads of heartbeats that never leave.
With every pulse, a bond we share,
In whispered dreams, beyond compare.

Through tangled paths, we find our way,
Each gentle touch, a soft ballet.
In colors bright, our lives entwined,
In the loom of hope, our hearts aligned.

Moments stitched with laughter's thread,
Through storms faced and tears we've shed.
In every beat, a tale we weave,
Of love's design, we dare believe.

As seasons change, our tapestry grows,
In every hue, our story glows.
Bound by the strands, forever strong,
In the threads of life, we both belong.

Song of Serendipity

In a world of twists and turns,
Fortune smiles, as the heart yearns.
Moments fleeting, softly collide,
In laughter's glow, fate's gentle guide.

Whispers echo through the air,
Chance encounters, little care.
Like petals carried by the breeze,
Hope blossoms in sweet unease.

Unexpected paths we tread,
With open hearts, leave doubts unsaid.
A dance of joy, the stars align,
In serendipity, love's design.

Alchemy of Hearts

In the crucible of dreams, we stand,
Transforming wishes with a touch of hand.
Silver threads and golden schemes,
We weave our hopes into the seams.

Embers glow in tender light,
Love's elixir, pure delight.
With every glance, the potion swells,
Two souls merging, magic spells.

Through trials fierce, we forge our way,
Holding close what words can't say.
In the alchemy of hearts, we find,
A bond unbroken, forever intertwined.

Echoes of Desire

In the shadows, longing grows,
A silent call that softly flows.
Whispers drift on nights so still,
Carried forth by passion's thrill.

Each heartbeat echoes loud and clear,
A symphony that draws us near.
In stolen glances, dreams ignite,
As we chase the fading light.

Through tangled thoughts, your name is sung,
A melody where love is sprung.
In echoes soft, our souls entwine,
In desire's dance, forever shine.

Flames of Connection

In the hearth of our embrace,
Fires flicker, time can't erase.
Warmth surrounds us, brightly glows,
In every heartbeat, love bestows.

With tender sparks, we light the night,
In this warmth, everything feels right.
Two souls igniting, freely soar,
As flames of connection yearn for more.

Through storms that may attempt to part,
These embers burn within the heart.
Together we will always stay,
In the flames forever play.

Frames of an Unseen Love

In whispers soft, we catch a gaze,
Moments shared, lost in the haze.
A touch that lingers, a silent wait,
Unseen threads weave our fate.

Like shadows dance upon the wall,
So closeness grows, yet fears befall.
Frames of time, where love resides,
In secret spaces, quietly hides.

Eye to eye, in fleeting sighs,
Unwritten words, where longing lies.
Within the silence, hearts confide,
An unseen bond, never to divide.

Hope unfurls in the muted light,
Two wandering souls, alight in night.
Unseen love, tender and bright,
In every moment, feels so right.

Bridges of Belonging

Across the river of hearts we glide,
Bridges built where dreams abide.
Hands entwined, a steady hold,
In the warmth, our stories unfold.

Paths can twist, yet still we find,
Home in places, undefined.
Each step forward, a tale to weave,
In every laugh, in all we believe.

Voices echo, a song of kin,
In the dance where we begin.
Unspoken truths in every glance,
Bridges of belonging, our sweet chance.

Through stormy skies and sunlit days,
Together we walk, in myriad ways.
For in connection, we are strong,
Bridges of love, where we belong.

Melting Heartbeats

In the chill of night, our hearts connect,
Like melting wax, we softly reflect.
Breath to breath, like whispers blend,
In the stillness, love ascends.

Moments pass like falling snow,
In tender flashes, feelings grow.
Every heartbeat, a gentle call,
Melting edges, we feel it all.

Underneath the starlit sky,
Our souls entwined, we float and fly.
Softly spoken, the dreams we share,
Melting heartbeats, laid so bare.

In every touch, a warmth ignites,
With quiet strength, love takes flight.
Through time and space, we echo sweet,
Melting heartbeats, forever meet.

Stars That Align

In the tapestry of night, they gleam,
Stars that twinkle, like whispered dreams.
Cosmic dance of fate unfolds,
In every heart, a story told.

Across the sky, our wishes soar,
Connected souls that yearn for more.
Every glimmer, a sign of grace,
Stars that align, our sacred space.

In the quiet, we feel the pull,
Hearts entwined, our minds so full.
A constellation of love so bright,
Guiding us through the darkest night.

With each moment, the universe sways,
In starry paths, we navigate ways.
Together, we find our destined role,
Stars that align, in every soul.

Embrace of Infinity

In the stillness of the night,
Stars whisper secrets bright,
Time flows like a gentle stream,
Wrapped in the cosmic dream.

Endless skies above our heads,
Where all our hopes and wishes spread,
Embracing moments yet to come,
In this expanse, we are home.

Eternity's soft, tender sighs,
Canvas painted with our ties,
We dance beneath the moon's soft gaze,
In love's embrace, forever stays.

With every heartbeat, we explore,
The universe opens its door,
Infinite paths that we can tread,
Together, by the stars we're led.

Winds of Change

Whispers in the rustling leaves,
Tell tales of what heart believes,
The winds carry dreams aloft,
Where hope begins to feel soft.

Seasons shift with gentle grace,
Nature wears a brand new face,
Change is constant, ever true,
Boldly we welcome the new.

Like waves upon the golden shore,
Together we will seek for more,
The breeze will guide us hand in hand,
As we journey through this land.

With every gust, we learn to fly,
Embracing horizons, we'll try,
The winds of change, they fan the flame,
Igniting courage without shame.

Shades of Togetherness

In the palette of our days,
Colors blend in gentle ways,
Brushstrokes of our laughter loud,
Canvas forming life's great crowd.

Each moment, a vibrant hue,
Shadows dance, and lights break through,
In this tapestry so fine,
We paint our love, forever shine.

Through the storms, we hold on tight,
Finding warmth within the night,
Together we stand, unafraid,
In each other, love's cascade.

With every brush of time that fades,
Strengthen bonds, our roots now laid,
Shades of truth in every glance,
Together, we embrace the chance.

Sails in the Sea of Love

We cast our dreams upon the tide,
With sails unfurled, we boldly ride,
The ocean whispers soft and low,
Guiding us where heartbeats flow.

In waves of laughter, tears collide,
Through storms we find the strength inside,
Each sunrise brings a brand new light,
In love's embrace, we hold on tight.

The horizon stretches far and wide,
Together as our hearts confide,
Adventures wait, the stars align,
Sails in the sea, your heart is mine.

With every gust, our spirits soar,
Navigating love's vast shore,
In the voyage, we discover,
Sails unfurl, we'll always hover.

Radiance of Togetherness

In the quiet glow of morning's light,
Hands entwined, everything feels right.
Words unspoken, yet hearts align,
Together we rise, two souls combined.

Through the storms and gentle rains,
Our laughter dances, easing pains.
Embracing change, we face the tide,
Radiance grows, with you beside.

Underneath the vast, endless sky,
Promises made, we will not deny.
In every heartbeat, a gentle grace,
In the warmth of love, we find our place.

As seasons shift, and moments pass,
In unity, a bond will last.
Together we shine, forever bright,
In the radiance of shared delight.

A Symphony of Us

Notes intertwine, a melody sweet,
Each heartbeat echoes, like a rhythmic beat.
In perfect harmony, we find our song,
Together composing where we belong.

Underneath the moonlight's tender gaze,
Our laughter dances in a playful haze.
A symphony played on strings of the heart,
Creating a masterwork, a beautiful art.

Every glance, a note that sings,
With every touch, new joy it brings.
In this orchestration, strong and true,
Our lives entwined, forever in view.

Through the crescendos and soft refrains,
In every struggle, love still remains.
Together we rise, our spirits soar,
In a symphony that's forevermore.

The Art of Falling

In the dance of dusk, when shadows blend,
We take a leap, and our hearts transcend.
With every stumble, we learn to trust,
In the art of falling, we find the just.

Leaves drift softly on an autumn breeze,
We embrace the chaos, the sweet unease.
Through the spirals and twists, we explore,
In every descent, we ask for more.

With courage stitched in every seam,
We rise through the ashes, igniting the dream.
Hand in hand, as we plunge and sway,
In the art of falling, we find our way.

So let us leap, with hearts open wide,
In love, in life, together we glide.
Each graceful tumble, a brush with fate,
In the dance of falling, we celebrate.

Kisses Beneath the Stars

Underneath the blanket of a twinkling sky,
Whispers of love flutter gently by.
Each kiss we share, a spark ignites,
In the stillness of night, our souls take flight.

With constellations bright, we weave our dreams,
In the silence, love's laughter gleams.
Hands entwined, we dance in grace,
Kisses beneath, a sacred space.

As the moonlight bathes our tender glow,
The world fades, and our hearts know.
In every moment, time stands still,
In your embrace, I feel the thrill.

So let us gather the stars above,
Kissing softly, unearthly love.
In the night’s embrace, we are free,
Kisses beneath, just you and me.

Astral Connections

In the night, stars twinkle bright,
Whispers of fate in cosmic flight.
Galaxies dance, a silent song,
Binding our hearts where we belong.

Waves of light from distant skies,
Carry our dreams as time flies.
Together we drift, a celestial race,
Lost in the vastness of timeless space.

Constellations weave tales untold,
In the universe, our spirits unfold.
Each spark ignites a cosmic thread,
Guiding us where our hearts are led.

When shadows fall and silence reigns,
The echoes of love forever remains.
In astral realms, we find our way,
Forever connected, come what may.

Tranquil Yet Tumultuous

In the stillness, chaos brews,
Gentle waves hide deep blues.
A calm facade, a raging heart,
In the silence, we drift apart.

Leaves rustle in the autumn breeze,
Echoes of love, like distant seas.
Tender hearts bear storms of fears,
Dancing shadows through the years.

Under the moon, secrets collide,
In tranquil dreams, we mask the tide.
Each ripple holds a tale so rife,
A dual dance of joy and strife.

Yet, in the turmoil, beauty gleams,
In the depths of our wildest dreams.
Together, a journey we brave,
Through peace and war, our hearts will save.

Horizons of Affection

Across the sea where sunlight fades,
Lies a world of welcoming cascades.
In every wave, a promise flows,
Boundless love, where the heart knows.

Mountains rise, kissing the sky,
In every breath, whispers sigh.
With every sunset, a glow ignites,
Embracing the warmth of soft moonlight.

Paths we tread, both new and old,
Unfolding stories waiting to be told.
Hand in hand, through valleys we roam,
In every step, we find our home.

Horizons stretch, endless and wide,
In your heart, I will forever abide.
With love as our guide, we'll fly high,
In the canvas of life, just you and I.

Puzzles of the Heart

Pieces scattered, lost in time,
Searching for reason, rhythm, and rhyme.
In every glance, a question stirs,
As the mystery of love blurs.

Each heartbeat echoes, a cryptic clue,
In silent moments, I see you.
Hidden paths where our spirits play,
Connecting the dots, come what may.

Fragments of dreams, a mosaic bright,
Casting shadows in the pale moonlight.
Together we fit, a tapestry spun,
In the puzzles of heart, we are one.

Through tangled thoughts and whispered prayers,
We navigate love's intricate layers.
In every piece, a soul's embrace,
Completing the puzzle, finding our place.

www.ingramcontent.com/pod-product-compliance
Ingram Content Group UK Ltd.
Pitfield, Milton Keynes, MK11 3LW, UK
UKHW020121171224
452675UK00014BA/1497

9 789916 873403